Exploring the World of Foxes

Copyright © 2020

All rights reserved.

DEDICATION

The author and publisher have provided this e-book to you for your personal use only. You may not make this e-book publicly available in any way. Copyright infringement is against the law. If you believe the copy of this e-book you are reading infringes on the author's copyright, please notify the publisher at: https://us.macmillan.com/piracy

Contents

Facts abouts Foxes 1

14 Fascinating Things About Foxes 12

The Exotic Arctic Marble Fox 27

Fenex Fox 29

Gray Fox 33

Sliver Fox 36

Arctic Fox 41

Cross Foxes 46

Facts abouts Foxes

The red fox is the most common and widespread fox species in the world, found throughout most of the United States.

Foxes are omnivorous mammals that are light on their feet. They are often mistaken for other members of the Canidae family, which include jackals, wolves and dogs. They stand out from their relatives because of their long, thin legs, lithe frame, pointed nose and bushy tail.

These animals are very social and live flexible lives. They are found all over the world — in North America, Europe, Asia and North Africa

— and call a wide range of terrains their home. They also eat a greatly varied diet.

Size

Most foxes are around the same size as medium-sized dogs. Since foxes are smaller mammals, they are also quite light. They can weigh as little as 1.5 lbs. (680 grams) and as much as 24 lbs. (11 kg). The fennec fox is the smallest living fox and doesn't get any bigger than a cat — about 9 inches (23 centimeters) and weighing 2.2 to 3.3 lbs. (1 to 1.5 kilograms), according to National Geographic. Other species can grow to 34 inches (86 cm) from their head to their flanks. Their tails can add an additional 12 to 22 inches (30 to 56 cm) to their length.

Habitat

Foxes usually live in forested areas, though they are also found in mountains, grasslands and deserts. They make their homes by digging burrows in the ground. These burrows, also called dens, provide a cool area to sleep, a good location to store food and a safe place to have their pups. Burrows are dug-out tunnels that have rooms for the fox and its family to live in. The burrows also have several exits so that they can flee if a predator enters the burrow.

Habits

Foxes are very social creatures that live in packs. A group of foxes are called a leash, skulk or earth, according to the U.S. Department of

Interior. They are also called packs. No matter what you call them, foxes like to stick near family members. A pack may include older siblings, foxes of breeding age, mates and mothers. Male foxes are known as dogs, tods or reynards, and females are called vixens.

These mammals like to hunt at night and are nocturnal. This means that they sleep during the day. This can change, though, depending on where the fox pack lives. If they live in a place where they feel safe, a fox pack may hunt during the daytime, according to National Parks and Wildlife Service of Ireland.

Foxes have great eyesight. They can see just as well as a cat, in fact. Their eyes are much like a cat's thanks to their vertically slit pupils.

Foxes are also very fast. They can run up to 45 mph (72 km/h). That is almost as fast as the blackbuck antelope, one of the world's fastest animals.

Diet

Foxes are omnivores. This means that they eat meat and vegetation. A fox's diet can consist of small animals, such as lizards, voles, rats, mice, rabbits and hares. They round out their diet with birds, fruits and bugs, according to the Smithsonian. Foxes that live near the ocean eat fish and crabs, as well. If they have trouble finding food, a fox will have no problem raiding trash cans to find scraps.

Foxes can eat up to several pounds of food a day. What they don't eat, they often bury under leaves or snow for later.

Offspring

Fox babies are called pups. During mating season, the female will cry out to let males know that she is ready. After mating, females will make a nest of leaves inside her burrow on which to have her pups. This special room in the burrow is called a nesting chamber.

The pregnant female only carries her pups for a gestation period of 53 days. There are usually two to seven pups in a litter. Pup care is a family affair. Both the mother and father share the care of pups. Even older siblings will help take care of their younger brother and sisters by bringing them food.

Foxes live very short lives in the wild. They often live only around three years, according to the Animal Diversity Web. In captivity, they can live much longer. Foxes in zoos, for example, can live 10 to 12 years.

A fox breeding program in Russia may help reveal the genetic roots of domestication of animals.

Classification/taxonomy

Foxes belong to several genera in the Canid family. Here is the taxonomy of foxes, according to Integrated Taxonomic Information System (ITIS):

Kingdom: Animalia **Subkingdom**: Bilateria **Infrakingdom**: Deuterostomia **Phylum**: Chordata **Subphylum**: Vertebrata **Infraphylum**: Gnathostomata **Superclass**: Tetrapoda **Class**: Mammalia **Subclass**: Theria **Infraclass**: Eutheria **Order**: Carnivora **Suborder**: Caniformia **Family**: Canidae

Genus/species: *Cerdocyon thous* (crab-eating fox)

Genus: *Lycalopex* **Species**:

Exploring the World of Foxes

- *Lycalopex culpaeus* (culpeo)
- *Lycalopex fulvipes* (Darwin's fox)
- *Lycalopex griseus* (South American gray fox)
- *Lycalopex gymnocercus* (pampas fox)
- *Lycapolex sechurae* (Sechuran fox)
- *Lycalopex vetulus* (hoary fox)
- **Genus/species**: *Otocyon megalotis* (bat-eared fox)
- **Genus**: *Urocyon* **Species**:
- *Urocyon cinereoargenteus* (gray fox)
- *Urocyon littoralis* (island gray fox)
- **Genus**: *Vulpes* **Species**:
- *Vulpes bengalensis* (Bengal fox)
- *Vulpes cana* (Blandford's fox)
- *Vulpes chama* (Cape fox)
- *Vulpes corsac* (Corsac fox)
- *Vulpes ferrilata* (Tibetan fox)
- *Vulpes lagopus* (Arctic fox)
- *Vulpes macrotis* (kit fox)
- *Vulpes pallida* (pale fox)
- *Vulpes rueppellii* (Rüppel's fox)
- *Vulpes velox* (swift fox)
- *Vulpes vulpes* (red fox)
- *Vulpes zerda* (fennec fox)

Conservation status

Most fox species are not endangered, according to the International Union for Conservation of Nature. The union's Red List of Threatened Species includes island gray foxes (near threatened), Sechuran foxes (near threatened) and Darwin's fox (threatened). It is estimated that there are fewer than 2,500 mature Darwin's foxes in their habitat in Chile. Domestic dog attacks and associated diseases are the main threats, the IUCN said.

Other facts

Foxes are usually monogamous. This means that they have only one mate for life. They also take on nannies to help with their pups. The nannies are female foxes that are not breeders. Sometimes, one male fox will have several female mates. Females that have the same male mate are known to live in the same den together.

Foxes can identify each other's voices, just like humans. The red fox has 28 different sounds they use to communicate. These vocalizations include yips, growls and howls.

The small, slender body of a Red fox allows it to run nearly 30 mph.

Fox hunting was a popular recreation sport in England since the 1500s. Hunting foxes without the aid of dogs is still practiced in the United Kingdom and several other countries including the United States.

In folklore, foxes are typically characterized as cunning creatures sometimes having magical powers.

In the wild, fox cubs can fall prey to eagles. Coyotes, gray wolves, bears and mountain lions are all predators for adult foxes.

Foxes have excellent hearing. They can hear low-frequency sounds and rodents digging underground.

14 Fascinating Things About Foxes

Foxes live on every continent except Antarctica and thrive in cities, towns, and rural settings. But despite being all around us, they're a bit of a mystery. Here's more about this elusive animal.

1. Foxes are Solitary.

Foxes are part of the Canidae family, which means they're related to wolves, jackals, and dogs. They're medium-sized, between 7 and 15 pounds, with pointy faces, lithe frames, and bushy tails. But unlike their relatives, foxes are not pack animals. When raising their young, they live in small families—called a "leash of foxes" or a "skulk of foxes"—in underground burrows. Otherwise, they hunt and sleep alone.

2. They have a lot in common with cats.

Like the cat, the fox is most active after the sun goes down. In fact, it has vertically oriented pupils that allow it to see in dim light. It even hunts in a similar manner to a cat, by stalking and pouncing on its prey.

And that's just the beginning of the similarities. Like the cat, the fox has sensitive whiskers and spines on its tongue. It walks on its toes, which accounts for its elegant, cat-like tread. And foxes are the only member of the dog family that can climb trees—gray foxes have claws that allow them to climb and descend vertical trees quickly. Some foxes even sleep in trees—just like cats.

3. The red fox is the most common fox.

Geographically, the red fox has the widest range of the more than 280 animals in the order Carnivora. While its natural habitat is a mixed landscape of scrub and woodland, its flexible diet allows it to adapt to many environments. As a result, its range is the entire Northern Hemisphere, from the Arctic Circle to North Africa to Central America to the Asiatic steppes. It's also in Australia, where it's considered an invasive species.

4. Foxes use the earth's magnetic field.

Like a guided missile, the fox harnesses the earth's magnetic field to hunt. Other animals, like birds, sharks, and turtles, have this "magnetic sense," but the fox is the first one we've discovered that uses it to catch prey.

According to *New Scientist*, the fox can see the earth's magnetic field as a "ring of shadow" on its eyes that darkens as it heads towards magnetic north. When the shadow and the sound the prey is making line up, it's time to pounce.

5. They are good parents.

Foxes reproduce once a year. Litters range from one to 11 pups (the average is six), which are born blind and don't open their eyes until nine days after birth. During that time, they stay with the vixen (female) in the den while the dog (male) brings them food. They live with their parents until they're seven months old. Vixens have been known to go to great lengths to protect their pups—once, in England, a fox pup was caught in a wire trap for two weeks but survived because its mother brought it food every day.

6. The smallest fox weighs under 3 pounds.

Roughly the size of a kitten, the fennec fox has elongated ears and a creamy coat. It lives in the Sahara Desert, where it sleeps during the day to protect it from the searing heat. Its ears not only allow it to hear prey, they also radiate body heat, which keeps the fox cool. Its paws are covered with fur so that the fox can walk on hot sand, like it's wearing snowshoes.

7. Foxes are playful.

Foxes are known to be friendly and curious. They play among themselves, as well as with other animals, like cats and dogs do. They love balls, which they will steal from backyards and golf courses.

Although foxes are wild animals, their relationship with humans goes way back. In 2011, researchers opened a grave in a 16,500-year-old cemetery in Jordan to find the remains of a man and his pet fox. This was 4000 years before the first-known human and domestic dog were buried together.

8. You can buy a pet fox.

In the 1960s, a Soviet geneticist named Dmitry Belyaev bred thousands of foxes before achieving a domesticated fox. Unlike a tame fox, which has learned to tolerate humans, a domesticated fox is docile toward people from birth. Today, you can buy a pet fox for $9000, according to Fast Company. They're reportedly curious and sweet-tempered, though they are inclined to dig in the garden.

9. Arctic foxes don't shiver until -70° celsius.

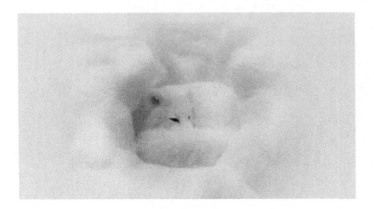

The arctic fox, which lives in the northernmost areas of the hemisphere, can handle cold better than most animals on earth. It doesn't even get cold until –70°C (-94°F). Its white coat also camouflages it against predators. As the seasons change, its coat changes too, turning brown or gray so the fox can blend in with the rocks and dirt of the tundra.

10. Fox hunting continues to be controversial.

Perhaps because of the fox's ability to decimate a chicken coop, in the 16th century, fox hunting became a popular activity in Britain. In the 19th century, the upper classes turned fox hunting into a formalized sport where a pack of hounds and men on horseback chase a fox until it is killed. Today, whether to ban fox hunting continues to be a controversial subject in the UK. Currently, fox hunting with dogs is not allowed.

11. They appear throughout folklore.

Examples include the nine-tail fox from various Asian cultures; the Reynard tales from medieval Europe; the sly trickster fox from Native American lore; and Aesop's "The Fox and the Crow." The Finnish believed a fox made the Northern Lights by running in the snow so that its tail swept sparks into the sky. From this, we get the phrase "fox fires" (though "Firefox," like the Mozilla internet browser, refers to the red panda).

12. Bat-eared foxes listen for insects.

The bat-eared fox is aptly named, not just because of its 5-inch ears, but because of what it uses those ears for—like the bat, it listens for insects. On a typical night, it walks along the African savannah, listening until it hears the scuttle of prey. Although the bat-eared fox eats a variety of insects and lizards, most of its diet is made up of termites. In fact, the bat-eared fox often makes its home in termite mounds, which it usually cleans out of inhabitants before moving in.

13. Darwin discovered a fox species.

During his voyage on the *Beagle*, Charles Darwin collected a fox that today is unimaginatively called Darwin's Fox. This small gray fox is critically endangered and lives in just two spots in the world: One population is on Island of Chiloé in Chile, and the second is in a Chilean national park. The fox's greatest threats are unleashed domestic dogs that carry diseases like rabies.

14. What does the fox say? a lot, actually.

Foxes make 40 different sounds, some of which you can listen to The most startling though might be its scream.

Fennec Fox

Physical Description

Their coats are long, soft, and thick and range in color from reddish cream to light fawn to almost white. Their undersides are pure white, and their tails are bushy with black tips.

These foxes are adapted to life in the desert. They have the largest ears relative to their body size of any member of the canid family, which they use to dispel heat and track down prey underneath the sand. They are also the palest of all foxes, giving them excellent camouflage. Heavily furred paws provide traction when running in the sand while also offering protection from the extreme heat of the terrain. Fennec foxes are also capable of going for long periods without consuming water; they are able to hydrate through the food they consume.

Size

The smallest of all canids, fennec foxes are 14 to 16 inches (35.6 to 40.6 centimeters) long, with an additional 7 to 12 inches (18 to 30 centimeters) of tail. They usually weigh between 2 and 3 pounds (0.9 to 1.4 kilograms). Perhaps their most notable characteristic is their ears, which can grow to between 4 to 6 inches (10.2 to 15.2 centimeters) in length.

Native Habitat

Fennec foxes live in North Africa, throughout the Sahara Desert and east to Sinai and Arabia. They prefer sandy deserts and arid regions with desert grasses or scrub vegetation.

Communication

Fennec foxes are territorial, and mark their terrain with urine and feces. Vocalizations among these foxes are common, and can manifest as whimpers, barks, shrieks, squeaks, growls, howls or chatters.

Food/Eating Habits

In the wild, fennec foxes eat insects—particularly grasshoppers and locusts—as well as small rodents, lizards, birds and their eggs. They will also consume roots, fruits and leaves, which help them to hydrate. Hunting occurs at night and alone; fennec foxes use their abnormally large ears to listen for prey underneath the sand, and once located will dig with all four feet to expose their meal. They can catch and kill prey larger than themselves; there have been documented cases of fennec foxes taking down fully grown rabbits.

At the Smithsonian's National Zoo, fennec foxes eat meat, assorted fruits and vegetables, mice and insects.

Social Structure

Monogamous animals, fennec foxes can live in family groups of up to ten individuals. There have been some instances of multiple family groups sharing a complex den.

Reproduction and Development

Fennec foxes typically give birth to one litter of pups per year, with between two and five young in a litter. During the four to six weeks of rutting season, males can become extremely aggressive and will mark their territory with urine. Females will go into estrus for one to two days, and following copulation the gestation period lasts between 50 and 53 days. Males defend females before and during birth, and will provide food to the female until the pups are about 4 weeks old. Young are born fully furred but blind; their eyes open after eight to 11 days, and they are able to walk at about 2 weeks. Pups usually nurse for their first 10 weeks of life and become mature at 9 to 11 months.

Sleep Habits

Nocturnal animals, fennec foxes will hide out in burrows during daylight to avoid the hottest portion of the day. They create the burrows themselves, often digging out a series of tunnels that can reach up to 32 feet (10 meters) in length. It is not uncommon for these dens to have multiple entrances and exits to provide a safe escape in the event of an outside threat.

Lifespan

Fennec foxes may live up to 11 years in human care.

The Exotic Arctic Marble Fox

The *coloration* of the Arctic Marble Fox is not something which occurs in nature but is acquired from human intervention and the kits are born in captivity. Marble foxes occur as genetic mutations, called *color phases*, resulting from breeding the red fox. Their beautiful white fur displays patches of black or tan across the face and on the ears. The *Fur Commission USA* also reports that an "arctic marble" was born in a *silver* fox litter in Norway in 1945 at Sverre

Ozzie, in the photo above, was rescued by the *Black Pine Animal*

Sanctuary after being left on the front porch of a home in Indiana without care. He was only about six months of age and had already lived a number of different places.

While *exotic* animals have become favorites to own, research and education on the species you wish to acquire is the very first step. Living with and caring for a fox is very *different* than owning a cat or dog. Check first to determine if owning a fox is legal in your state. We had sugar gliders for a number of years, and discovered that it is not legal in every state to have a sugar glider living in your home. Learn the facts about the fox or any exotic animal before you make that purchase.

Do your research to find reputable dealers. As with all *breeders/dealers*, some are just in it for the money without respect to the animal or its welfare. Foxes are not going to

thrive while living in a house on a full-time basis. They are outdoor animals and also need an outdoor *environment* in which to feel at home. Their life span is typically 10 to 15 years in captivity and they will weigh anywhere from 6 to 20 pounds. The first six months of a fox kit's life is the ideal time to develop *bonding*. Foxes need activity and attention to avoid boredom as a bored fox will find something to do and it will probably tend toward being more destructive. *Diet* for a fox can include beef, venison, poultry, fruit, vegetables, and dog food. Concern has to be given to other animals you may have. Dogs and foxes tend to get along very well, but cat's and foxes are not a good mix. When adding another kit to mix, it is best to monitor any activity between the two until the kit becomes older. Litter box training can take longer with some foxes than others, but *persistence* is the key to success. Unless you plan on breeding your fox, spaying/neutering will diminish some of odor arising from their marking. They will continue to mark their territory even after spaying/neutering.

Gray Fox

Identification

Length: Adult gray foxes can be up to 47 inches in length.

Weight: Adult gray foxes vary in weight from 6 to 15 pounds.

Color: Gray fox have coarse, salt and pepper gray hair with black markings on the head, nose and muzzle. They will also have a medial black stripe down the top surface of the tail with a black tip.

Sounds: yapping, howling, barks, whimpers and screams.

Habitat

Range: Gray fox can be found from southern Canada to northern Venezuela (South America), excluding the northwestern United States. They tend to stay away from urban areas, preferring a more secluded habitat.

Diet: They are opportunistic foragers that will eat virtually every kind of meat, fruit, vegetable or insect. Their favorite meals are small mammals, especially cotton-tail rabbits.

Status: Least Concern (population stable). Fairly common in southeastern counties of MN.

Gray Fox climbing a tree. Image from *ItsNature.org*.

Gray Fox tracks. Image from *Bear-Tracker.com*.

Life Cycle

Reproduction: Gray fox mate in February or March. Gestation lasts about 52 days with 3 to 7 kits born in April/May. The young open their eyes at 10 days, and will venture out of the den after about 4 weeks. At 10 weeks, they are usually weaned, with the father providing solid food for the entire family. They will all remain together until late fall, but will generally be solitary during the winter.

Adaptations: Gray fox are unique in the canid family, in that they are one of two species of canid that climb trees. They have rotating wrists and semi-retractable claws that help them climb up high to den, forage, or escape predators. This is a risky behavior for these fox, as they are not great at climbing down, and can easily injure themselves in the process.

Gray fox are also sometimes known as the "tree fox" or the "cat fox". Their pupils are oval shaped, rather than slit-like. These fox are common, but very elusive and rare to spot in the wild. They are primarily nocturnal, but may forage during the day.

Silver Foxes

The silver fox is a melanistic form of the red fox. They may represent about 10% of the red fox population. The silver fox's coloration can range from black to bluish gray to silver with a white-tipped tail. Silver hairs may be widely scattered all over their body. Their pelt is prized in the fur industry and thus, they are raised on farms for fur production. They have a thick dark undercoat with an outer coat which may be 2 inches longer than the undercoat. Their fur is soft and glossy and the soles of their feet are thickly coated.

Life span

Red foxes have a lifespan of 3 years in the wild and 10 to 12 years in captivity.

Diet

Silver foxes are opportunistic hunters and eaters. They prefer a carnivorous diet but can rely on plant material when meat is scarce. In the wild, they use different strategies to hunt different prey. When they hunt small animals, they rely on sound to locate the prey and then spring up to pin the victim to the ground and kill by biting it. For larger ground prey, they rely on stalking and rapid pursuit. Catty Shack's silver fox eats 3-5 pounds of food 5 or 6 nights a week. The Catty Shack Ranch follows the USDA guidelines and feeds according to their body weight. They also follow strict nutrition requirements from their veterinarians and also add vitamins and minerals to all their food.

Size

Red foxes may range from 17 to 35 inches long (head and body) with a tail from 12 to 22 inches long. They may weigh 6 to over 20 pounds. Females are usually smaller than males.

Habitat & numbers

Silver foxes may be found over much of the northern hemisphere and even in Australia. Humans introduced them to many habitats for hunting purposes. In North America, they are found mostly in the Northwest although historically they were trapped in the East. In Russia, they are found predominantly in Siberia and in the Caucasus mountain region.

Reproduction

In the wild, silver foxes do not necessarily mate only with similar colored individuals. They can mate with other red foxes or individuals who are silver/red mixes. In captivity, they are bred to others of the same color. Silver foxes reach sexual maturity by 10 months of age. Mating occurs once a year, usually in January and February. Males and females are generally seasonally monogamous during the mating season. Gestation is about 52 days and litters can range from 1 to 14 pups, averaging 3 to 6 pups. Larger litters occur when the mother is more mature and when food is abundant. The male will help provide food for the mother and pups and helps protect the den. Unmated females will also help raise a large litter. The pups venture outside the den at 4 to 5 weeks of age and are weaned by 8 to 10 weeks of age. They remain with their mother until their first autumn.

Arctic Fox

Region: Arctic

Destinations: Bear Island, Greenland, Svalbard, Iceland

Name: Arctic Fox (a.k.a White Fox, Snow Fox, Polar Fox) (*Vulpes lagopus*)

Length: 75 to 100 cm (including tail)

Weight: 3 to 8 kg

Location: The Arctic

Conservation status: Least Concern

Diet: Small animals, carrion, fish, birds, berries, seaweed, insects, small invertebrate

Appearance: White in winter, brown (brown/white spotted) in summer. About 10% of the population stays dark during winter and is termed "Blue fox". His type was particularly valuable to the trappers during the trapper period.

How do Arctic Foxes Hunt?

Foxes will eat just about anything they can get their paws on. During summers lemmings will often be the main part of their diet, but they'll also go after birds, eggs, and even seal pups. The fact that their coats change colour the year round means they are always camouflaged and able to sneak up on prey. With its wide (but short) ears an Arctic Fox can hear its prey moving under snow. Once it has located its next meal, the fox will pounce straight up then down right on top of their victim. In the fall they'll work hard to store up body fat, increasing their weight by up to 50%. During winter, when food becomes much more scarce, the foxes will often follow polar bears around and then scavenge what they can off of a kill once the bear is done.

Do they socialize?

Arctic Foxes are generally independent until they mate, which means their territory has fewer mouths to feed come winter.

How fast can Arctic Foxes move?

Arctic Foxes are quite fleet when they want to be, sprinting up to nearly 50 km per hour.

What are Arctic Fox mating rituals like?

Breeding season occurs during April and May, when foxes will mate in monogamous pairs. The couple will either dig out a new den, or move into a pre-existing one. These dens can often contain a long network of tunnels covering as much as 1000 m^2. The pregnancy lasts about 52 days when a litter of 5-10 offspring, called "kits," are born. Both the mother and the father are present to help raise the young. The kits first emerge from the den about a month after being born, and are weaned off their mother's milk after a further 4 or 5 weeks.

How long do Arctic Foxes live?

Arctic Foxes generally live from 3 to 6 years.

How many Arctic Foxes are there today?

There isn't a solid number regarding Arctic Foxes, though they're estimated to be in the hundreds of thousands. Their population fluctuates depending on the availability of food sources, especially the lemming population. However the populations of Finland, Norway, and Sweden is estimated to be only about 120 adults.

Do they have any predators?

Grey Wolves were traditionally the biggest predator Arctic Foxes had to face. But because of global warming the territories of Artic Foxes and Red Foxes are overlapping, causing a new and increasing threat to Artic Foxes. Artic Foxes were a mainstay of fur trappers thanks to their luxuriously warm and beautiful coats.

7 Fascinating Facts about Arctic Foxes

- Arctic Foxes have one of the warmest mammal fur in the world.
- They have short stubby legs in order to keep them low to the ground and out of the cold Arctic winds.
- They have small noses, eyes, and ears as an additional caution against the cold.
- They have fur on the bottom of their feet which keeps them from slipping on the ice.
- Arctic Foxes are so well-adapted to handle the cold that they can endure temperatures as low as -50 degrees Celsius before their metabolism kicks in to try to heat the body from within.
- Artic Foxes are the smallest member of the *canid* family found in the wild in Canada.
- Arctic Fox burrows can have dozens of entrances and have sometimes housed generations of foxes.

Cross Foxes

There are many interesting types of foxes, different species, color mutations, and more. The cross fox is one of the coolest of them all!

Cross foxes are red foxes (Vulpes, Vulpes) that have a partially melanistic color morph. The melanin causes the red fox to have a strip of dark fur down its back and across its shoulders that cross.

The cross fox is a fox that stands out to most people. It's beautiful and it's unusual colors make us marvel at them.

We've put together this list of facts that you probably didn't know about this mysterious creature.

At one point scientists thought that this fox was its own species, but it was later found that they were **red foxes that had a mutation.**

Cross Foxes Are Red Foxes With A Color Morph

The cross fox is one of the coolest looking foxes. What many people may not know is that they are actually a red fox with a partial **melanin color variation** or color morph.

Red foxes have more than one color morph.

A cross fox is created when a red fox morph mates with a silver fox morph, and sometimes two silver foxes can also produce these types of foxes.

They all fall under the red fox species, (Vulpes, Vulpes) however, **the cross fox was once thought to be a different species** of fox called (Canis decassatus.)

What Is Melanin?

Melanin is a color mutation that happens in the skin, that **makes the skin and hair a dark color**. Cross foxes have partial melanin, where some of the black/dark pigments meet the usual lighter colors.

Silver foxes also are melanistic and have more of the mutation than the cross fox does, making them almost completely black and some with very silver colors.

Albinoism is the opposite of melanin, where the skin and hair do not have any dark pigments.

Melanin is a mutation that exists in many animals and species, even in human beings.

Where Do Cross Foxes Live?

Cross foxes live mainly in North America, in the northern regions, such as Canda and northern America.

Many of these foxes live in Canada and around 30% of their red fox populations have this mutation.

There were cross foxes in the northern united states such as in Utah, but it is believed that the fur trade wiped them out of those areas for the most part.

They have also been seen in parts of Europe such as Scandinavia, and Finland.

Habitats and Behavior

Cross foxes have pretty much the same behaviors as the common red fox. Since **cross foxes live primarily in the northern regions** they are no strangers to snow and cold conditions.

They dig dens to have their kits and they sleep mostly outside in wooded areas. Their habitats consist of a den with multiple openings and sometimes even multiple dens spread out across its home range.

They are preyed on by large raptor birds, bears, and other animals that live in the northern territories.

Cross foxes that are urban are a little rarer, but there have been photographs of them crossing roads and venturing close to town.

Are Cross Foxes Rare?

Believe it or not, cross foxes are really not that rare. They make up for around 25% of all red fox variations in North America.

Their pelts were once more sought after by trappers and fur farms when it was thought that they were a different species than a red fox variation.

In Europe, there is a smaller amount of red foxes with the cross fox variation. In Finland, a study of 3,000 pelts found that only a tiny percentage of non-red variations foxes had the mutation.

Cross Fox Description

The cross fox has the shape of a red fox, although some have claimed that they are slightly bigger. They have a mixture of red and dark-colored fur, as well as some white fur.

They have a little bit more fur under their feet so that they can walk on snow and ice in the northern climates, similar to Arctic foxes.

There is more than one type of **cross fox morph**, which differs from the genetics of the parents.

The dark color goes down their back and to the tail, and across the shoulders. The red/orange color comes through in patches.

Cross Fox Tail

The tail on this fox is slightly more bushy than a common red fox variation. They are usually black with some orange or silver guard hairs showing through.

The tail can be a medley of black, orange, and white.

All cross foxes have white-tipped tails, just like red foxes, and silver foxes.

There can be some color variations with the tail as well as some unusual coloring.

A fox's tail is used for communication. They signal other foxes with different signs, such as to be alert, or that they have buried food.

Cross Fox Morphs and Variations

The standard cross fox is a mix of black, orange, and white. However, there are some other variations of the color morph.

Color variations:

- **Standard/common**
- **Gold cross**
- **Silver cross**

The **standard cross fox** has a slightly lighter color variation than the other two morphs. With a lighter silver/black coat along with a lighter orange.

The gold variation is darker than the standard or common cross fox. The orange is a golden orange or even fire red. These are rarer than the standard.

The silver cross variation has a completely black body with orange around the ears and the cheeks. This is the rarest of these three.

All of these variations of white-tipped tails.

There are other cross fox color variations caused by recessive mutations.

Cross Fox Baby

Since there is a smaller percentage of these mutations, the babies are rarer than common red fox ones in the wild.

The common **cross fox is created when a red fox mates with a silver fox**.

It is believed that cross foxes have a similar gestation period as the red fox. Which is around 49 – 58 days.

They are usually born a light black color, or brown.

Their babies are just like any other red fox, they are fed by their parents until they can fend for themselves. They are taught to forage and to how to hunt after they venture out of the den.

Conclusion

The cross fox has been misunderstood for a very long time. It's easy to see why they became victims of fur farms and trappers.

Their fur was once worn by holy men and priests and designated as an item of importance.

Cross foxes may not be as rare as some people think, however, they do possess a **unique color morph** that inspires the imagination.

It doesn't take much for me to get excited about foxes but every time I see one of these beautiful foxes I can't help but feel like nature has its very own paintbrush that makes everything on this planet unique.